Coloring book for adults and kids amazing squirrel image for design

This coloring book is belongs to

____

____

____

www.ingramcontent.com/pod-product-compliance
Lightning Source LLC
Chambersburg PA
CBHW081319250726

48662CB00008B/2653